MODERN ROLE MODELS

Soulja Boy Tell 'Em

Karen Schweitzer

Mason Crest Publishers

Produced by OTTN Publishing in association with
21st Century Publishing and Communications, Inc.

MASON CREST PUBLISHERS INC.
370 Reed Road
Broomall, Pennsylvania 19008
(866) MCP-BOOK (toll free)
www.masoncrest.com

Printed in the United States of America.

First Printing

9 8 7 6 5 4 3 2 1

Library of Congress Cataloging-in-Publication Data

Schweitzer, Karen.
  Soulja Boy Tell 'Em / Karen Schweitzer.
    p. cm. — (Modern role models)
  Includes bibliographical references.
  ISBN 978-1-4222-0509-9 (hardcover) — ISBN 978-1-4222-0796-3 (pbk.)
  1. Soulja Boy, 1990–   —Juvenile literature. 2. Rap musicians—United States—Biography—Juvenile literature. I. Title.
ML3930.S69S39 2008
782.421649092—dc22
[B]   2008025055

Publisher's note:
All quotations in this book come from original sources, and contain the spelling and grammatical inconsistencies of the original text.

CROSS-CURRENTS

In the ebb and flow of the currents of life we are each influenced by many people, places, and events that we directly experience or have learned about. Throughout the chapters of this book you will come across **CROSS-CURRENTS** reference boxes. These boxes direct you to a **CROSS-CURRENTS** section in the back of the book that contains fascinating and informative sidebars and related pictures. Go on. ▸▸

CONTENTS

Rapper Soulja Boy Tell 'Em started out recording music and putting it on the Internet to have fun with his friends. He ultimately launched a nationwide dance craze, climbed music charts in multiple countries, and helped change how the entertainment industry discovers and markets new talent—all before his 18th birthday.

1

Soulja Boy Tell 'Em

SOULJA BOY TELL 'EM HAS ESTABLISHED HIMSELF as a major player in the music industry. Before he was 18 years old, the young rapper attracted a legion of fans and created the biggest dance craze since the Macarena. But Soulja Boy Tell 'Em is more than just an artist who can write catchy **beats**—he's also an **entrepreneur**.

Unlike most musicians, Soulja Boy Tell 'Em was famous before he got his first record deal. This self-made star started out as an online sensation. He used various Web sites, like YouTube and MySpace, to introduce himself and his music. Within a matter of months, Soulja Boy Tell 'Em had developed a huge following online. People from all over the world were downloading his songs and his videos and sharing them with friends.

➤ How It All Started ⬅

Soulja Boy Tell 'Em developed an interest in music early on. At the age of 12, he got his first computer and used it to pursue that interest. A friend had taught him how to produce his own beats, and a cousin gave him a computer program that allowed him to record his own songs.

Not long after, Soulja Boy Tell 'Em began rapping, collaborating with friends, and putting the songs he made on SoundClick, a Web site that allows artists to rate each other's music. He didn't expect anything to come from it initially, but then something happened that would change the course of his life: other people began to give him good ratings.

Soulja Boy Tell 'Em decided to take it a step further. He created a MySpace page, a YouTube account, and his own Web site. He became more and more visible online. In March of 2007, Soulja Boy Tell 'Em recorded a song called "Crank That" and posted it on the Internet.

➤ "Crank That" ⬅

Deciding that he needed something visual to go along with the new song, Soulja Boy Tell 'Em also recorded a short video that featured him doing the "Soulja Boy" dance. The dance moves weren't new—he was doing them before he ever wrote the words to "Crank That"—but the dance fit the song well.

To his surprise, "Crank That" was an overnight success. Soulja Boy Tell 'Em began to receive record-breaking page views on MySpace. People were also visiting YouTube regularly to check out the video. Within a few months radio stations were playing "Crank That" at regular intervals, and people all over the world were doing the Soulja Boy dance.

In August 2007, the self-published song was used on an episode of *Entourage*, a popular television series on HBO. Two weeks later, Soulja Boy Tell 'Em was invited to the set of MTV's *TRL* to perform and demonstrate the Soulja Boy dance.

➤ Soulja Boy Visits *TRL* ⬅

Total Request Live, more commonly known as *TRL*, is a television series on the MTV network that features the ten most requested music videos. Daily guests, like musicians, actors, and actresses, also stop by to promote current projects.

Soulja Boy Tell 'Em performs the ultra-catchy song and dance that helped make him famous. After thousands of fans filmed themselves attempting to mimic his "Crank That" routine and posted the footage online, he created an instructional video breaking down the dance into easy steps.

SOULJA BOY TELL 'EM

Being invited to *TRL* is an honor for any entertainer, because the show is not only very popular, but influential as well. It has been credited with helping the careers of teen artists like Britney Spears, Christina Aguilera, and Jessica Simpson.

Soulja Boy Tell 'Em appeared on *TRL* for the first time on August 27, 2007. While he was there, he performed "Crank That" in front of a live audience and showed actress Natalie Portman

Soulja Boy Tell 'Em arrives at MTV's Times Square Studios in New York City on August 27, 2007, ready for his first appearance on *TRL*. He says he began writing his name on sunglasses with correction fluid to amuse his classmates in high school, but never guessed that the sunglasses would become his signature fashion statement.

how to do the Soulja Boy dance. Natalie was on the show to promote her latest film, *Mr. Magorium's Wonder Emporium.*

When she heard that Soulja Boy Tell 'Em was backstage, she encouraged him to come out and give her an **impromptu** dance lesson. The crowd went wild when he arrived on set. They continued to cheer as they watched Natalie try to execute the Soulja Boy dance moves while wearing high heels.

The *TRL* appearance helped make Soulja Boy Tell 'Em even more famous than he was before. Within days, "Crank That" began to climb music charts all over the world.

CROSS-CURRENTS
To find out more about the place where TRL is filmed, read "MTV's Times Square Studio." Go to page 48. ▶▶

⇒ CHART TOPPER ⇐

"Crank That" hit the coveted number one spot on the *Billboard* Top 100 Chart on September 15, 2007. The song remained there for two weeks before being overtaken by "Stronger," a song by Kanye West. On October 6, "Crank That" moved back into the number one spot and stayed there for five more weeks.

The song also held the number one spot on most of *Billboard's* other music charts, including Hot Rap Tracks, Hot Ringtones, Pop 100, and Hot Digital Songs. It peaked at number three on *Billboard's* Hot R&B/Hip-Hop Songs.

CROSS-CURRENTS
Read "What Is the Billboard Hot 100?" to learn more about what Soulja Boy Tell 'Em's chart accomplishment means. Go to page 49. ▶▶

"Crank That" enjoyed international success as well. The song was in the top ten on well-respected music charts all over the world, including the UK Singles Chart, the Canadian Top 100, the UK R&B Singles Chart, the Irish Singles Chart, the New Zealand Top 40, and the United World Chart.

While some people were surprised by the **unprecedented** success of "Crank That," nobody was more shocked than Soulja Boy Tell 'Em, who said afterwards:

❝'Crank That' was just a song that I was fooling around with and recorded. I never would've thought the song could have gotten that big, so I'm happy and blessed that it did what it did.❞

DeAndre Cortez Way—now better known as Soulja Boy
Tell 'Em—poses in a homemade T-shirt, 2006. The
young rapper has lived in the South for most of his life,
spending his formative years in Atlanta and in Batesville,
Mississippi. His simple but clever music reflects the
region's musical trends.

2

Growing Up
in the South

SOULJA BOY TELL 'EM WAS BORN IN CHICAGO, Illinois, on July 28, 1990. His parents, Traci Jenkins and Carlisa Way, named him DeAndre Cortez Way. It was his mom who gave him the nickname "Soulja Boy." As for the rest of his name, Soulja Boy explains it this way:

> **"When I started rapping, in every song I'd say, 'Soulja Boy tell 'em' in the beginning of the song and that really just stuck with me. My fans called me that. So basically I just kept that name."**

When he was six, Soulja Boy Tell 'Em left Chicago and moved to Atlanta, Georgia, with his mother and his younger brother. Life was tough for the young rapper. His family had very little money, and growing up poor was hard on everyone in the family. Soulja Boy Tell 'Em used schoolwork as a distraction. He was a straight A student throughout elementary school and into middle school.

Music also provided an outlet. The music scene in Atlanta was red hot at the time. Popular artists from the area, like OutKast and Usher, were rising to fame. Inspired, Soulja Boy Tell 'Em began hanging out with Young Kwon, a friend who knew how to produce beats and record songs.

Soulja Boy Tell 'Em reveals on his Web site that he learned a lot from Young Kwon:

> **"He was the one who taught me how to make beats and record; he recorded the first songs I ever did. He taught me what he knew about snap beats in the studio in his house."**

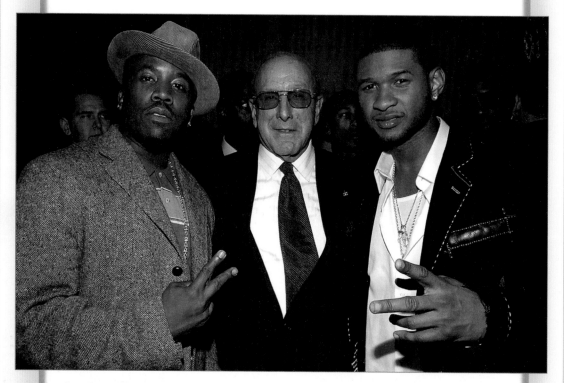

Soulja Boy Tell 'Em developed his career in Atlanta, home of a musical scene that helped the city earn the nickname "Hot-lanta." Other musicians who moved to Atlanta to launch their careers include Big Boi of the rap duo OutKast (left) and R&B singer Usher (right). In the center is Clive Davis, CEO of the RCA Music Group.

⇒ MOVING TO MISSISSIPPI ⇐

Before entering high school, Soulja Boy Tell 'Em moved to Batesville, Mississippi, to live with his father. The move was financially driven. Traci had some money and could provide more for his son than Carlisa could.

The move was difficult for Soulja Boy Tell 'Em, who was only 14 years old at the time. It ended up being just what he needed, however, to take his music to the next level. Commenting on it later, he said:

> **"When I went to Mississippi, I had to adjust to what was going on. But it was really a blessing in disguise, because if I would've never moved to Mississippi I wouldn't be where I'm at today. I wouldn't have had access to no computer, no internet, no camera to film my dancing."**

While he was in Mississippi, he formed a group with his best friend Abrahim Mustafa (better known as "Arab"). They called themselves Dem 30/30 Boyz. Together, the two friends performed songs in a recording studio that Traci provided.

Soulja Boy Tell 'Em also began to produce his own beats with a computer program that his cousin had given him. At first it was all in fun, but then he noticed that he was getting better and better at it.

⇒ TAKING IT TO THE WEB ⇐

Now that he had access to the Internet, Soulja Boy Tell 'Em decided to put his music online. Some of the first videos he produced and uploaded were **parodies** of other popular songs. But then, he began to produce original music, which he uploaded to SoundClick.

SoundClick is a Web site that hosts music. Both signed and unsigned musicians—that is, musicians with or without recording contracts—use this site to promote their songs. Soulja Boy Tell 'Em didn't expect the songs to catch on. As he told *Billboard* magazine:

CROSS-CURRENTS

To find out about other singers who have attracted notice after posting their music on the Internet, read "YouTube Singing Sensations." Go to page 50. ▶▶

> **"** Really I was just playing around, but after I uploaded the first song, I was rated well. The SoundClick site linked to my MySpace page and my hits started increasing, so I started taking it seriously. **"**

Soulja Boy Tell 'Em set up his own Web site, www.souljaboytellem.com, to help promote his name. He also founded his own record **label**: Stacks on Deck Entertainment, which has signed artists like Jbar, Arab, and S.O.D. Money Gang. It wasn't long before his business started working and people started talking.

⇒ BACK IN ATLANTA ⇐

In 2004, Soulja Boy Tell 'Em went back to Atlanta to work on his music. He partnered with a manager, who helped him with his career. Not long after, Soulja Boy Tell 'Em was booked for his first live performance.

He performed three songs on a stage in Indiana. Although he was extremely nervous, he managed to put on a great stage show. The success led to more live performances in other cities.

Soulja Boy Tell 'Em also continued to put his songs and videos on the Internet. People from all over the world were keeping track of him on Web sites such as YouTube and MySpace.

⇒ "CRANK THAT" ⇐

Throughout 2006, Soulja Boy Tell 'Em worked on his first independent album, *Unsigned and Still Major*. He wrote, performed, and produced all of the songs. In March 2007, he released a single called "Crank That," as well as a video that showed him dancing to the song.

CROSS-CURRENTS

Read "Using MySpace to Get Famous" for some tips and suggestions about how people can promote themselves online.
Go to page 50. ▶▶

"Crank That" was an instant success on the Internet, and within two months, the catchy tune was also being played on the radio. Mr. Collipark, a producer who was looking for new talent, heard the single and decided to check out Soulja Boy Tell 'Em's MySpace page. He was shocked to see that more than ten million people had decided to do the same thing.

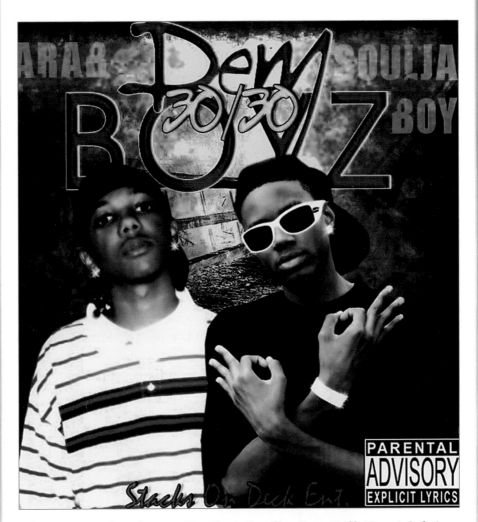

The cover of a demo CD that Soulja Boy Tell 'Em (right) and Arab recorded independently in 2006 as Dem 30/30 Boyz. The two friends still work together today. Soulja Boy Tell 'Em features Arab in many of his songs and videos. Soulja Boy even named a song, "Pass it to Arab," after his friend.

Mr. Collipark was sure the numbers must be fake, so he started asking around about the rapper. When he realized that Soulja Boy Tell 'Em was the real thing—a genuine Internet phenomenon—he contacted the rapper immediately. Soulja Boy Tell 'Em was signed to Interscope Records within weeks.

Soulja Boy Tell 'Em performs in Atlanta in September 2007, shortly before his debut album on Interscope Records was released. By this time, the video for "Crank That" had been viewed millions of times. Although Soulja Boy's success seemed to come out of nowhere, it was the result of hard work and good business instincts.

3

From Online Sensation to Superstar

AT ONLY 16 YEARS OLD, SOULJA BOY TELL 'EM was not only an online sensation, he was also a self-made millionaire thanks to his Interscope record deal. Everyone from Beyoncé Knowles to Samuel L. Jackson was doing the Soulja Boy dance. The young rapper was on top of the world. But the best was yet to come.

Shortly after signing him, Interscope arranged a video shoot for "Crank That," the song that would be the first single on Soulja Boy Tell 'Em's new album. The music video featured a cameo by music producer Mr. Collipark. Other artists like Arab, Bow Wow, Omarion, Jibbs, Baby D, Unk, and Rich Boy also appeared in the "Crank That" video to demonstrate the Soulja Boy dance.

CROSS-CURRENTS

Read "Other Interscope Artists" to learn about some other musicians who are signed to Soulja Boy Tell 'Em's label. Go to page 51. ▶▶

Soulja Boy Tell 'Em said later that the debut of his TV music video was thrilling beyond words:

> **"The most exciting moment of my career was the first time I saw myself on TV. It was the 'Crank That' music video. I was just sitting at home, and Interscope called me and said, 'We're going to premiere the video today.' I was sitting on the couch and telling everybody, 'I'm gonna be on TV!' When it came on, I couldn't explain how it felt. It was the best feeling in the world."**

⫸ *SOULJABOYTELLEM.COM* ⫷

When Soulja Boy Tell 'Em went into the studio to create his first album with Interscope, his goal was to make sure that each song was good enough to be a single. He had gotten serious about his music career at this point and wanted to make sure that he didn't become a **one-hit wonder**.

The title he chose for his first album was *Souljaboytellem.com*. He figured it would be a good way to promote his Web site. The name also served as a tribute to his Internet roots. The Internet had made him famous, and he appreciated it.

Soulja Boy Tell 'Em took charge while he was in the studio, making the decision to produce most of the **tracks** on the album. The bold choice certainly seemed to pay off. *Souljaboytellem.com* sold a very respectable 117,000 copies its first week. The album also debuted at number 4 on the *Billboard* Top 200.

Not surprisingly, Interscope was very happy with the success of *Souljaboytellem.com*. Their latest artist had worked very hard and made the company a lot of money. Mr. Collipark commented publicly on how impressed he was with Soulja Boy Tell 'Em:

CROSS-CURRENTS

To learn more about another influential group that Mr. Collipark has produced, read "The Ying Yang Twins." Go to page 52. ▶▶

> **"The more I'm around the kid, the more I see how special he is. I think he's the future of the way music's going. Coming into the game, he's done all the work for the record company who's trying to find**

an artist with substance and an existing fan base. The game right now is based on somebody lucking up and finding a hit record, but that somebody has no substance. Soulja Boy Tell 'Em comes with that substance already built in. 99

➢ CRITICIZED ➣

Critics did not embrace *Souljaboytellem.com* in the same way fans had. At the time of its release, the album received more bad reviews than good. The most common complaint was its repetitive lyrics. It was bad enough that some reviewers dismissed Soulja Boy as a one-hit wonder. A critic at *Entertainment Weekly* went a step further by ranking *Souljaboytellem.com* as the "worst record of 2007."

The catchiness of Soulja Boy Tell 'Em's music has attracted listeners of all ages, many of whom first learned about him thanks to his clever use of viral marketing. As a result, he already had a fan base by the time his major-label debut album, *Souljaboytellem.com*, dropped on October 2, 2007.

Accompanied by friend and collaborator Arab and producer Mr. Collipark, Soulja Boy Tell 'Em poses on the red carpet before the 2007 BET Hip-Hop Awards, which took place on October 13, 2007 at the Atlanta Civic Center. During the ceremony Soulja Boy Tell 'Em performed "Crank That," which won the award for Best Hip-Hop Dance.

Despite the negative reviews, the album was incredibly successful. The first single from *Souljaboytellem.com*, the dance hit "Crank That," held the number one spot on the *Billboard* Hot 100 chart for seven weeks and dominated other music charts around the world. The single also set a historical record by making Soulja Boy Tell 'Em the first artist to sell more than 3 million downloads of a digital song online.

"Crank That" also became a stadium anthem. It was frequently played at least once during NFL games, NBA games, and other sporting events. The song was especially popular at college games and school functions. Sports players, fans, and mascots loved dancing in unison to the "Crank That" beat.

Soulja Boy Tell 'Em, his music, and his dance were such a hit that he was often invited to perform at NFL sporting events and college games. One team, the Cleveland Browns, even filmed a promo spot with him to get people to watch their games.

⇒ THE REAL DEAL ⇐

If his time on music charts didn't convince people that Soulja Boy Tell 'Em was a real success, the awards that he received for "Crank That" did. The song was nominated for a Grammy Award for Best Rap Song in December of 2007. Some of the other artists nominated in the best rap song category the same year included hip-hop powerhouses like Kanye West and 50 Cent. In the end, Soulja Boy Tell 'Em lost to Kanye West. But being nominated for the award was validation enough.

Awards that Soulja Boy Tell 'Em did win for "Crank That" include the Best Hip-Hop Dance Award from BET and the Dirty Award for Best Dance Song. The song was also number 21 on *Rolling Stone*'s list of the Best Songs of 2007, number 14 on MTV's Best Songs of 2007, and number one on BET's Top 100 Music Videos of 2007.

⇒ THE SOULJA BOY DANCE ⇐

Although the "Crank That" song was successful all on its own, the official Soulja Boy dance that went along with the catchy tune certainly helped draw attention to Soulja Boy Tell 'Em and his music. Everyone wanted to learn how to do the Soulja Boy dance. In August of 2007, the rapper made it easier by creating an instructional video that demonstrated how to do the dance properly.

The video was filmed in the same waterless swimming pool that was featured in the *Stomp the Yard* movie. With the help of a few friends, Soulja Boy Tell 'Em broke down every move and then posted the video on the YouTube Web site. The instructional video accumulated more than 30 million page views in only six months time, making it more popular than the original "Crank That" video.

Several other video versions could be found on the site as well. For months, fans had been uploading their own homemade video clips to the Internet. More than 40,000 versions of the Soulja Boy dance had been posted to YouTube by September 2007. Some of the video clips even featured animated characters like SpongeBob SquarePants, Dora the Explorer, Barney, Bambi, Winnie the Pooh, the Lion King, and the Simpsons "cranking it" to the Soulja Boy Tell 'Em tune.

In addition to dance videos, "Crank That" also spawned both official and unofficial song remixes. Artists like Lil' Wayne, Twista, Jermaine Dupri, and Short Dawg all participated in remix versions of the song. "Crank That" was also redone by rocker Travis Barker, who added a guitar and called it the "Travis Barker Remix."

Other versions of the song include "Crank Dat Batman," "Crank Dat Spider-Man," and "Crank Dat Aquaman." The "Crank Dat Batman" remix was one of the most successful, receiving significant airplay on both radio and television.

⇛ LAWSUIT ⇚

Shortly after his album was released, Soulja Boy Tell 'Em ran into some legal trouble. Another rapper, who went by the name Souljah Boy, filed suit against the "Crank That" rapper. Soulja Boy Tell 'Em's record label, attorney, and manager were also named in the lawsuit.

William Lyons, a.k.a. Souljah Boy, claimed that he had the stage name Souljah Boy first. Lyons had been using the name for 12 years and felt that Soulja Boy Tell 'Em was infringing on the trademark.

Reps for Soulja Boy Tell 'Em responded immediately after the lawsuit was filed to try to settle the matter out of court. They were also quick to point out to the media that Soulja Boy's full artist name was Soulja Boy Tell 'Em.

⇛ CAUSING CONTROVERSY ⇚

The lawsuit filed by William Lyons was not the only problem Soulja Boy Tell 'Em faced that year. The lyrics of his song, "Crank That," also caused **controversy**. There were rumors surfacing on the Internet claiming the song contained inappropriate sexual innuendo.

Soulja Boy Tell 'Em performs during the So So Def Summer Fest's Celebrity Basketball Game at the Georgia State College Arena in Atlanta, July 2007. Behind him, his longtime friend Arab serves as his hype man—a backup performer who accompanies a rapper and encourages the audience to get excited about the show.

Soulja Boy Tell 'Em insisted to the media that the lyrics were being misunderstood:

> ❝They've got it all wrong. People like to say my songs are sexual and that really gets to me. That could hurt my reputation and affect the future of my career. People are just misinterpreting the lyrics. ❞

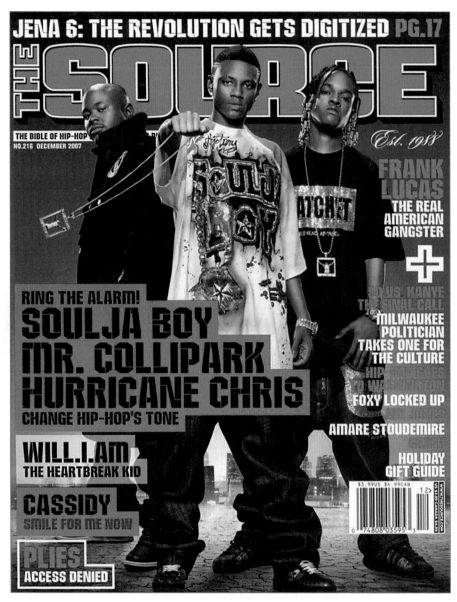

JENA 6: THE REVOLUTION GETS DIGITIZED PG.17

THE SOURCE

Est. 1988

THE BIBLE OF HIP-HOP
NO.216 DECEMBER 2007

RING THE ALARM!
SOULJA BOY
MR. COLLIPARK
HURRICANE CHRIS
CHANGE HIP-HOP'S TONE

WILL.I.AM
THE HEARTBREAK KID

CASSIDY
SMILE FOR ME NOW

PLIES
ACCESS DENIED

FRANK LUCAS
THE REAL AMERICAN GANGSTER

PLUS. KANYE THE FINAL CALL

MILWAUKEE POLITICIAN TAKES ONE FOR THE CULTURE

HIP HOP GOES TO WASHINGTON

FOXY LOCKED UP

AMARE STOUDEMIRE

HOLIDAY GIFT GUIDE

$3.99US $4.99CAN

0 74808 03595 3

Producer Mr. Collipark (left) and two of his discoveries, Soulja Boy Tell 'Em and Hurricane Chris (right), on the cover of the December 2007 issue of hip-hop magazine *The Source*. Both Soulja Boy Tell 'Em and Hurricane Chris were just teenagers when they became stars, and they both consider themselves representatives of today's playful, club-friendly Southern hip-hop.

One thing that wasn't misinterpreted was the use of the word "ho" throughout the song. There were many school dances and skating rinks that banned "Crank That" after parents complained about the lyrics. The bans caused a huge debate in school newspapers across the country.

Some people thought that banning the song from any venue was a form of censorship. Other people thought that young kids shouldn't be listening to music with questionable lyrics—particularly on school property.

Soulja Boy Tell 'Em felt bad about the controversy and some of his choices. He admitted later in an interview that he had regrets about referring to women as "hos" in his songs:

> **"That's how I was raised, but it's not something I'm proud of. Since I've been in the music industry I've learnt from older people that it's not good to talk like that. I'm more careful now."**

➤ SOULJA GIRL ⬅

Soulja Boy Tell 'Em collaborated with several artists on his debut album, including the newly formed R&B trio i15. The track that i15 helped Soulja Boy Tell 'Em perform was "Soulja Girl," the second single released from the *Souljaboytellem.com* album.

The collaboration was a top 40 hit in the United States and in other countries, but it didn't enjoy the same success as Soulja Boy Tell 'Em's first single, "Crank That." At the height of its popularity, "Soulja Girl" reached number 32 on *Billboard*'s Hot 100 chart, number six on *Billboard*'s Hot Rap Tracks chart, and number nine on *Billboard*'s Hot Ringtones chart. The song also achieved modest success internationally, peaking at number 10 on the New Zealand Top 40 and number seven on the Canadian Hot 100.

Soulja Boy Tell 'Em's producer, Mr. Collipark, eventually remixed "Soulja Girl" to transform it into a song that people could dance to. The remix became a club favorite and was a huge hit on the Internet.

While he enjoys boasting about his self-made success, Soulja Boy Tell 'Em also acknowledges that hip-hop's trailblazers paved the way for him and all of today's young artists. The earliest hip-hop came from New York City in the late 1970s, followed by California's West Coast rap in the 1980s. Southern rap emerged as a distinct genre in the late 1990s.

Hip-Hop Trends

IN HIS OWN WAY, SOULJA BOY TELL 'EM IS A hip-hop pioneer. He has demonstrated a remarkable talent not just at making music and dance moves but at working the Internet. He managed to make a name for himself with little more than a computer, an Internet connection, and a video recorder.

Had it not been for his own efforts and innovative **viral marketing** campaign, Soulja Boy Tell 'Em may have never been a star. The success he has achieved may end up paving the way for other young artists who want to break into hip-hop. Several record producers have taken to the Internet hoping to find the next Soulja Boy Tell 'Em. A modest amount of equipment and a desire to make it big is all some aspiring artists need to become the next big thing.

Soulja Boy Tell 'Em recognizes the role he has played in all of this, but he also acknowledges that there were other hip-hop artists who paved the way for him first. In an interview with MTV, he said:

"They'll say I opened up a lot of doors for people. The first person who started this, what we call hip-hop, opened the door for me. It probably wasn't a party track or a 'Crank That,' it probably was something way, way, way different than what I'm talking about, but he still opened the door for what I'm doing, and if I never would have did this, [the next] wouldn't come. **"**

⇒ HIP-HOP AND ITS ROOTS ⇐

Some people say hip-hop began in the 1970s, but the earliest and most basic forms actually originated in Africa. Those who were ripped from that continent and forced into the cruel institution of slavery were the real mothers and fathers of hip-hop.

These proud humans refused to give up their spirit and dignity even as they were forced to perform backbreaking labor for other people. To stay strong, they chanted, sang songs, and beat out rhythms with their feet, hands, and any object that could be turned into a musical instrument. The music they made was one of the earliest forms of hip-hop.

⇒ THE RISE OF HIP-HOP ⇐

In the early 1970s, a Jamaican-born man nicknamed Kool Herc began to DJ dance parties throughout the Bronx in New York City. The parties were frequently held at Herc's home, in dance halls, on basketball courts, in the street, or anywhere there was spare space.

It was at one of these parties that Kool Herc introduced a traditional form of Jamaican poetry that is recited while music is played in the background. He also developed a completely new way of deejaying using turntables, speakers, and microphones. It wasn't long before other New York DJs began to copy his style and expand on it. Within months, a new form of music was born.

In the 1960s, singers like James Brown—and their producers at record companies like Atlantic and Motown—had already begun blending gospel, jazz, and rhythm-and-blues to create a new sound called soul. Another fresh musical style known as funk was also gaining in popularity at that time. Funk relied on **groove** and rhythm instruments, particularly the guitar, to make a beat you could dance to.

Kool Herc, James Brown, and other forward-thinking artists all helped pave the way for later hip-hop performers. Their music, their lifestyle, and their attitude were a major influence on the hip-hop music and **culture** we know today.

⇛ HISTORICAL HIP-HOP FIGURES ⇚

Kool Herc had a friendly rivalry with another DJ named Afrika Bambaataa. Frequently called "The Father of The Electro Funk Sound," Bambaataa is also considered one of the earliest pioneers of hip-hop. He had a style that was similar to Kool Herc's, but with a

Fab Five Freddy (left), Afrika Bambaataa (second from left), and DJ Kool Herc (right) attend the opening of a Smithsonian Institution exhibit on hip-hop, February 28, 2006. The director of the New York City museum's Behring Center for American History, Brent D. Glass (second from right), accompanies these founding fathers of hip-hop.

twist. Bambaataa used break-beat deejaying to mix together funk, rock, television shows, and other types of recordings.

Like Kool Herc, he too hosted block parties. The two deejays sometimes battled one another at sound system competitions. It was all very friendly, though. Bambaataa firmly believed that hip-hop should be about peace, unity, love, and having fun. This belief, as well as the work he did as an artist, helped spread rap and hip-hop culture throughout the nation and around the world.

Some of the DJs and other artists who started out shortly after Kool Herc and Bambaataa include Grandmaster Flash, Grandmaster

At a 2005 celebration of hip-hop history in New York City, DJ Grandmaster Flash performs his pioneering cutting technique. Born Joseph Saddler and raised in the Bronx, he was the frontman for Grandmaster Flash and the Furious Five. The group's 1982 single "The Message" is widely considered one of the most influential hip-hop songs of all time.

Caz, and DJ GrandWizzard Theodore. DJ GrandWizzard Theodore accidentally created the scratch technique one day when his mom was talking to him. He was trying to hold a spinning record in place to hear her better. The sound it made was so interesting that he decided to combine it with his other turntable tricks. Grandmaster Flash is credited with being one of the first DJs to **cut** records on a turntable, and Grandmaster Caz is famous for incorporating rap into his turntable work.

⇒ GOING MAINSTREAM ⇐

Before hip-hop was actually called hip-hop, it was known as disco rap. "Hip-hop" most often applies to music though it is also associated with dance, clothing, art, and the culture associated with these artistic forms. There is some disagreement as to who actually coined the term *hip-hop*. Some people say it was Lovebug Starski, who used it to describe the culture associated with the music. Others credit rapper Keith Cowboy, who used the term during stage performances early in his career.

Regardless of who made up the name, hip-hop hit the mainstream by the early 1980s. Artists like Kurtis Blow, Afrika Bambaataa and the Soul Sonic Force, Grandmaster Flash and the Furious Five, and the Sugar Hill Gang were drawing national attention. One of the singles released by the Sugar Hill Gang became a Top 40 hit, something that was unheard of at the time. Hip-hop was definitely on the move.

Hip-hop and rap had also spread to the West Coast, thanks to music videos and films that showcased hip-hop culture. Too Short, Ice-T, and other early West Coast rappers were all dabbling in a new style of music that would eventually be known as gangsta rap. Female artists like Salt-n-Pepa and MC Lyte were also making it big on the hip-hop scene.

Other aspects of hip-hop culture were starting to take hold at the same time. Breakdancing was popular in nearly every city of the country. Graffiti artists were leaving their **tags**

CROSS-CURRENTS

Read "Female Hip-Hop Artists" to learn about some of the most influential women in hip-hop history.
Go to page 53. ▶▶

in urban and rural areas alike, and hip-hoppers everywhere were learning how to use their voices and sound equipment to become human beatboxes.

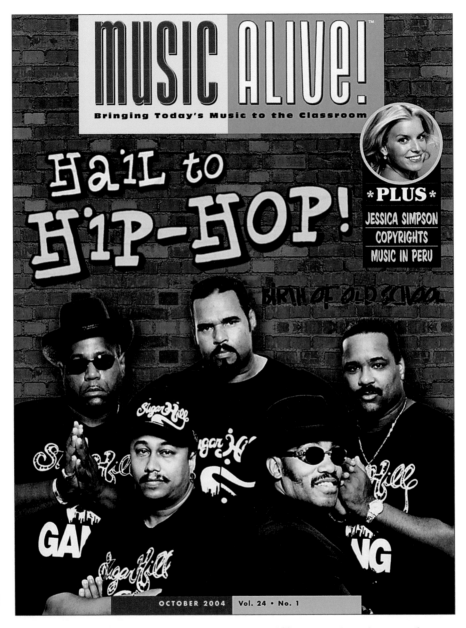

The pioneering rap group Sugar Hill Gang is pictured on the cover of this 2004 magazine. The group's 1979 song "Rapper's Delight" drew attention to an emerging style of music: hip-hop. "Rapper's Delight" was the first hip-hop song to become a mainstream hit, reaching number 36 on the Billboard pop music chart.

The cover of Salt-n-Pepa's fourth album, which included the hit singles "Shoop" and "Whatta Man." The groundbreaking female rap group was composed of MCs Cheryl "Salt" James and Sandra "Pepa" Denton, along with DJ Deidre "Spinderella" Roper. Salt-n-Pepa was the first female rap group to win a Grammy Award and to sell a million albums.

⇛ CONTEMPORARY HIP-HOP ⇚

By the 1990s, hip-hop had emerged from the underground to become one of the most popular forms of music in the world. Pop artists frequently borrowed from hip-hop, and rappers like Dr. Dre, Tupac Shakur, Snoop Dogg, and Jay-Z were burning up the charts.

The 2000s brought more changes and new influences. Eminem rose to fame, and new artists like 50 Cent, Diddy, and Kanye West became some of the biggest names in music. This decade also saw the

CROSS-CURRENTS

To find out about a genre of hip-hop music that is growing in influence, check out "Southern Hip-Hop." Go to page 54. ▶▶

hip-hop community come together to discuss some of the issues that plague the industry, such as racism and the **denigration** of women.

One of the most historic moments occurred when talk show host Oprah Winfrey arranged a "town hall meeting" with music mogul Russell Simmons, civil rights leader Dr. Benjamin Chavis, record executive Kevin Liles, and rapper Common to discuss the language used in some hip-hop songs. During the meeting, Dr. Chavis admitted that change is needed:

> **"**Hip-hop is not perfect. We've got to make it better. But we make hip-hop better by making society better, because hip-hop reflects the contradictions of society. There's too much poverty, there's too much injustice and there's too much bad treatment of women in our society.**"**

Shortly after the meeting, the Hip-Hop Summit Action Network released a statement requesting that recording and broadcast industries voluntarily remove racial slurs and derogatory comments toward women from hip-hop songs. While this hasn't completely eliminated the use of certain words, it certainly showed that leaders of the hip-hop community are eager to make hip-hop better.

⇒ A New Trend in Hip-Hop ⇐

One of the other new trends to emerge in hip-hop involves the music itself. Modern artists are focusing more on creating songs you can party and dance to versus songs that tell a life story. Part of the reason for this is that party jams are successful. They do well on the charts, on the Internet, and on the radio.

Simplistic, catchy songs also prosper in the music industry's hottest new market: cellular **ringtones** and **ringbacks**. These mobile music applications account for approximately 15 percent of the money most record companies earn. Their business used to be built on selling albums, but the potential in the mobile music market is just too big to ignore.

As king of the ringtone market, Soulja Boy Tell 'Em has been featured in numerous articles on the topic. Some have implied that

Sean Combs originally made his name as a producer, boosting the careers of hip-hop and R&B artists like the Notorious B.I.G. and Mary J. Blige. Under the name Puff Daddy, which he shortened to P. Diddy or simply Diddy, he achieved success as a rapper in his own right during the 1990s and early 2000s.

Some established hip-hop artists and journalists worry that music by trendy new artists like Soulja Boy Tell 'Em will damage hip-hop, because it is not as serious or complex as what came before it. Soulja Boy Tell 'Em dismisses their concerns, saying that his music is for young people and that his older critics may simply be out of touch.

he is just a "flavor of the month" versus an artist with real staying power. Their skepticism may be justified.

There have been many ringtone high-flyers like Soulja Boy Tell 'Em who have had one catchy song climb the charts. The problem is that they have a difficult time repeating that first success.

Veteran hip-hop artists are quick to point out reasons for this. In a recent interview with the Associated Press, Snoop Dogg commented on ringtone rappers:

"They're not making substance material—they're not really going into creating a sound. It's all about making the hot song for right now, but the artists who will stand the test of time like myself are about making records, not songs. You got to make a quality album so you can hold people's attention. It's like a movie. If you make a movie that got [only] one good scene, ain't nobody gonna go see it."

Many people, including artists, producers, and hip-hop fans, would agree with Snoop Dogg's statement. Other people appreciate the new trend, however, including record producer Mr. Collipark, who calls Soulja Boy Tell 'Em a real entertainer:

"He has a better chance of selling a million records than a lot of established artists do. Whether we as adults get it or not doesn't matter; it's a fact that he's already selling out shows by himself—headlining across the country. He's really an entertainer."

Judging by the ambitious goals he has expressed, Soulja Boy Tell 'Em is excited and optimistic about his future in the entertainment industry. Still, he plans ahead instead of living recklessly. He says he set aside the first earnings from his record deal in a trust fund, and hired a tutor to continue his education while on tour.

What the Future Holds

SOULJABOYTELLEM.COM WAS THE BESTSELLING hip-hop album of 2007, with more than 800,000 copies sold **domestically**. The album's smash single, "Crank That," set records by selling over 3.4 million downloads and nearly 3 million ringtones. Soulja Boy Tell 'Em also had the most viewed Web site of any artist, drawing in more than a million unique visitors each month.

The money was rolling in, and Soulja Boy Tell 'Em couldn't have been more pleased. After growing up in a poor household, it was exciting to have ample cash on hand to buy whatever was needed. Some 17 year olds would have been content with this fact—some would have even spent their money faster than they made it—but not Soulja Boy Tell 'Em.

He knew that keeping his fans interested in him, his music, and his entire business was a must if he wanted to continue to work in the hip-hop industry. After achieving success with "Crank That," he had this to say:

> **❝In this business, you have to have a plan. I'm going to take advantage of every opportunity I can while I'm hot and while everybody knows who I am. Maybe in four months from now, I won't have a 'Crank That' song that's taking over everything, and the same people who are looking at me today, probably won't be looking at me then.❞**

Soulja Boy Tell 'Em did take advantage of every opportunity that came his way. He made appearances on talk shows, performed at awards shows, and talked to nearly every newspaper and magazine that requested an interview. He also worked tirelessly to promote his name and grow his brand.

⟫ SOULJA STORE ⟪

Soulja Boy Tell 'Em decided that one of the best ways to promote himself was through his own line of products. With the help of Interscope Records, he launched the Soulja Boy Tell 'Em Store online. The store featured CD's, posters, t-shirts, and accessories like jewelry, key chains, and hats.

One of the most intriguing offerings was a two-piece set that consisted of a pair of black sunglasses and a white pen. Soulja Boy Tell 'Em was famous for wearing sunglasses that had his name written on them in white and thought he would give fans a chance to own their own pair of trademark shades.

CROSS-CURRENTS

If you would like to learn more about how rap stars have influenced the fashion world, read "Hip-Hop Fashion." Go to page 55. ▶▶

The glasses instantly became one of the most popular items in the store. Within weeks of putting them on the Web site, Soulja Boy Tell 'Em was selling 100 pairs of shades every single day.

⟫ YAHHH! ⟪

Shortly after launching his online store, Soulja Boy Tell 'Em released a third single from *Souljaboytellem.com*. Titled "Yahhh!", the song didn't have a dance to go along with it, but it did have a catchy beat. Soulja Boy Tell 'Em's old partner Arab helped out with the vocals

In summer 2008, the clothing company Yums announced that it had signed Soulja Boy Tell 'Em to create a line of clothing, shoes, and accessories. The rapper has never hidden his interest in fashion. His lyrics often mention what he likes to wear when making an impression. For example, his song "BAPES" is about the joys of buying new sneakers.

and also appeared in the music video, which debuted on BET the same month.

"Yahhh!" was an expression that Soulja Boy Tell 'Em and Arab had used for years as a way of saying "leave me alone" or "get out of my face." The video's story featured Soulja Boy Tell 'Em skipping class and being followed by all sorts of fans, including Britney Spears, Hillary Clinton, and Dog the Bounty Hunter.

The video was popular on the Internet, but the song did not have the same success as "Crank That" or "Soulja Girl." Nevertheless, it had a respectable showing for a third single. "Yahhh!" peaked at number 48 on the *Billboard* Hot 100 chart and at number 25 on *Billboard* Hot Digital Songs chart. It also appeared on several international charts, including the New Zealand Top 40, the Canadian Hot 100, the Irish Singles Chart, and the UK Singles Chart.

At the same time "Yahhh!" was getting airplay, Soulja Boy Tell 'Em could also be heard on the Collipark remix of Fergie's song "Clumsy," as well as the Tyra B song, "Get It Poppin'." He was also featured on songs by Trackstar, V.I.C., Lil Will, Arab, and Camp 22.

➤ HEADLINER ◀

Studio work was fun, but what Soulja Boy Tell 'Em really enjoyed was touring. He had been working the stage since he was 15 years old and enjoyed the response that he could get out of a crowd of fans.

In late 2007 and early 2008, he was the opening act for the Up Close and Personal Tour with Bow Wow and Chris Brown. His act was short—only 20 minutes long—but the crowds went wild every time he stepped on the stage. When the UCP tour ended, Interscope Records announced that Soulja Boy Tell 'Em would be headlining 21 and Under, a 23-city tour that would also feature Lil Mama, V.I.C, and Tiffany Evans.

Soulja Boy Tell 'Em told *Billboard* magazine that the tour was a thank you to all of his fans:

> **"It's been an incredible journey and I can't thank everybody enough for all the love and support they've shown me. I want to continue to give my fans what they want, a tour with the hottest young stars in music."**

Soulja Boy Tell 'Em was very appreciative of the support his fans had given him, and he let them know it constantly. When he wasn't busy with the tour, he spent a great deal of his time interacting with fans. He also continued to post videos on YouTube and was active on his blog and MySpace page.

On Souljaboytellem.com, fans were encouraged to submit photos, create personal profiles, and chat with one another on a community forum. When "Yahhh!" was released, Soulja Boy Tell 'Em also asked fans to send in their videos explaining what made them want to "Yahhh!"

➤ INSPIRATION ➤

As important as his fans were to him, they weren't the only motivation that Soulja Boy Tell 'Em had. In 2008, he told a reporter that it was 50 Cent who inspired him to reach greater heights:

> **"I'd say coming into the game, 50 Cent was the biggest inspiration on my career, because of everything he accomplished. I thank him just for being there, for me to look up to.""**

This bus advertises the October 2007 release of *Souljaboytellem.com*. Soulja Boy Tell 'Em attracted the attention of his first fans with innovative self-promotion, and has earned their loyalty by communicating with them on his interactive Web site. He even allows fans to send him personal greetings through e-mails and text messages.

SOULJA BOY TELL 'EM

Soulja Boy Tell 'Em has expressed admiration for fellow rapper Curtis Jackson, better known as 50 Cent. 50 Cent's breakthrough hit, "In da Club," became one of 2003's biggest songs. Combined, his first two albums alone sold over 21 million copies. 50 Cent originally promoted his music with homemade mixtapes, an approach similar to Soulja Boy's Internet marketing.

50 Cent is one of the most popular rappers in the world. He has sold millions of records worldwide and has been nominated for nearly 100 different awards. 50 Cent has also managed to establish successful enterprises outside his phenomenal rap career.

He starred in *Get Rich or Die Tryin'*, a semi-autobiographical account of his life, and has made appearances in a number of other movies. 50 Cent also has his own record label, his own clothing line, and two of his own video games. In 2007, he co-wrote a novel called *The Ski Mask Way* and collaborated with another author to write *The 50th Law*.

Some of 50 Cent's other business ventures include a book imprint, a film production company, and a line of vitamin water. In 2007, he sold the vitamin water business to Coca-Cola for $4.1 billion and announced that he would be launching a dietary supplement company.

50 Cent has demonstrated time and time again that there is no limit to what one person can do. It is easy to see why Soulja Boy Tell 'Em would be impressed by his role model's many accomplishments.

➤ BACK TO SCHOOL ◄

Soulja Boy Tell 'Em knew how much a hip-hop artist could achieve from watching 50 Cent, but he also knew how fleeting success could be. He released two singles after "Yahhh!", but neither did well on the charts. The first song, "Let Me Get 'Em," peaked at number 115 on the *Billboard* R&B chart and never made it on to any of the other charts. The second, titled "Donk," made it all the way to number 106 on the *Billboard* R&B chart, but it never climbed any higher.

Soulja Boy Tell 'Em decided that if he wanted to stay on top of the hip-hop game, he would need to strike again while the iron was still hot. In May of 2008, he announced to MTV that he would be releasing a second album:

❝My new album is called *Back to School*. Basically, it is really me taking it back to the basics. It's time to start studying again. Make it happen, man. . . . The time I drop the album, everybody is gonna be going back to school. My fans are 21 and under. That's what I'm focusing on.❞

SOULJA BOY TELL 'EM

Soulja Boy Tell 'Em didn't offer a release date for *Back to School*, but he did indicate that he had a marketing plan to make sure that the album was a success. He also mentioned that he would be working with a respected producer and was open to collaborating with other artists.

Soulja Boy Tell 'Em and Arab clown around for the camera during a performance on the British program show *Sound* on March 3, 2008. As he works on new music and explores his options in the worlds of acting, fashion, and animation, Soulja Boy Tell 'Em hopes to keep his fans happy.

⇒ WHAT THE FUTURE HOLDS ⇐

Soulja Boy Tell 'Em may be new to hip-hop, but he has already made a lasting impression on fans and the industry at large. Nobody will ever be able to forget 2007, the year that "Crank That" had everyone doing the Soulja Boy dance.

And if Soulja Boy Tell 'Em has his way, people will see a lot more of him in the future. In his spare time, Soulja Boy Tell 'Em wants to explore acting and computer animation. He has always been interested in the latter career especially, and he has even experimented with it for fun in the past.

He is currently working on a feature-length film that is based around the "Crank That" video, as well as a cartoon called *Bad Little Homies*. The cartoon will be about the adventures Soulja Boy Tell 'Em has with his friends. Other projects that are in the works include a clothing line and a signature shoe line. Meanwhile, in 2008 *Forbes* magazine, one of the most respected and influential business publications in the world, declared that Soulja Boy Tell 'Em was the "Hottest New Music Star."

With the kind of entrance he has made into the world of hip-hop, Soulja Boy Tell 'Em has been compared with other major forces in the

CROSS-CURRENTS

Read "Hip-Hop Artists in Films" to learn about some artists who have made the transition from music to movies." Go to page 56. ▶▶

world of music, dance, and video. In fact, *Souljaboytellem.com* has been held up to Michael Jackson's *Thriller* album and the singles and videos it spawned, all of which had a huge impact on music and popular culture in the 1980s. Whatever else Soulja Boy Tell 'Em decides to do, he will almost certainly continue to grow his brand and inspire other people to "Crank That."

MTV's Times Square Studio

MTV's studio is located at One Astor Plaza, a 54-story-high skyscraper in the heart of New York City's Times Square. The MTV studios are split into three separate studios named after different sections of Manhattan.

The Uptown Studio and the Midtown Studio are used for the *TRL* show. *MTV News* uses the Midtown Studio as well. The Downtown Studio is reserved for many of MTV's other shows. It is also used as a lounge for guests.

Times Square is a major intersection in Manhattan, so there is plenty to see. The first things visitors tend to notice are the thousands of digital advertisements that pepper every available bit of space. Building owners in Times Square are actually required to display billboards or neon signs!

Two of the most famous buildings in the neighborhood include One Times Square, where the New York Times Square Ball is dropped every year on New Year's Eve, and the Bank of America Tower, which is the second-tallest building in New York City after the Empire State Building.

During the busiest parts of the day, Times Square is so congested that pedestrians sometimes have to walk in the streets with cars. At any time of the day, if you spend enough time there and look hard enough, you are bound to see a famous face. (Go back to page 9.) ◀◀

MTV's Midtown and Downtown studios in Times Square, New York City. Each studio of MTV's Times Square headquarters features decorated window shades, instantly recognizable to the channel's viewers who gather outside. When the daily video countdown TRL is filming, fans can look for their favorite musicians and other celebrities who appear on

What Is the *Billboard* Hot 100?

Compiled weekly by *Billboard* magazine, the Hot 100 is a chart of the 100 most popular singles. Song rankings are based on sales, as well as radio airplay in more than 140 U.S. markets.

Billboard magazine was launched in 1894 under its original name, *Billboard Advertising*. The magazine was created to report industry news to poster printers, advertising professionals, and bill posters. As the years passed, the publication changed its editorial direction a number of times, as well as its name. By the 1930s, the pages of *Billboard* were filled with film, radio, and music industry news.

In the 1940s, the magazine published the Best Selling Retail Records chart, which tracked sales of the most popular music recordings. That chart was eventually combined with the Most Played by Jockeys chart (another list *Billboard* put out a few years later) to become the *Billboard* Hot 100.

Although many charts have come out since, the Hot 100 is considered the standard measure of popularity in the music industry.

In fall 2007, Soulja Boy Tell 'Em's "Crank That" topped the Billboard Hot 100 for seven weeks. It also hit the number one spot on other Billboard music rankings, including Hot Rap Tracks and Hot Ringtones. Billboard magazine contains each week's Hot 100. This issue, from June 16, 2007, features a cover story on R&B singer Chris Brown.

Getting a song on this chart, particularly in the top 10, is a major accomplishment for a musician.

(Go back to page 9.)

YouTube Singing Sensations

Soulja Boy Tell 'Em isn't the only singer to make a name for himself on YouTube. Many unsigned musicians use this video hosting Web site to have fun and to get noticed. Two of the most notable YouTube singing sensations are Esmee Denters and Marie Digby.

Esmee Denters

Esmee is a Dutch singer who began using a webcam in 2006 to post videos of herself on YouTube. In the beginning, she sang songs that were made popular by other pop artists, but she eventually began to post videos of original songs.

It wasn't long before Esmee got noticed and signed by Tennman Records. Since then, she has released several singles and opened concerts for Justin Timberlake. She has also performed on *The Oprah Winfrey Show*.

Marie Digby

Marie is an American singer who found fame on YouTube after posting a video that featured her performing Rihanna's song *Umbrella*. The version created by Marie found its way onto the radio and eventually made it to the number 10 spot on the Bubbling Under Top 100 Singles Chart.

She has performed the song on television several times and has since released her own single. Marie's debut album, *Unfold*, was dropped in 2008 and sold more than 18,000 copies in its first week.

(Go back to page 13.)

Using MySpace to Get Famous

MySpace was created so that people could socialize with one another online. The site is often used for that purpose, but it also serves as a promotional tool for entertainers and entrepreneurs.

Why Promote on MySpace?

MySpace is one of the most popular Web sites in the world. More than 200,000 people register for an account each day, which means that the site is constantly growing.

Having a MySpace page has become more important than having your own "dot-com" Web site, according to the American Society of Composers, Authors and Publishers (ASCAP). So many new and established artists are using MySpace to upload songs and sell music that the company has designed special "profile pages" for musicians.

Tips for Promoting Yourself on MySpace

If you are thinking about using MySpace to promote your work and build business contacts, you should plan your efforts carefully. A few things to keep in mind:

- Your MySpace page should look professional.

- Answer all questions and messages promptly and courteously.

- Getting fans and friends takes time. Most people don't become an overnight success on MySpace.

- Don't give too much personal information away—your safety should be your number one priority.

(Go back to page 14.)

Other Interscope Artists

Other artists besides Soulja Boy Tell 'Em who are signed to Interscope Records include the following:

Dr. Dre

Dr. Dre isn't a medical professional as his name suggests. He helped pioneer gangsta rap in the 1980s and since earned the reputation as one of the greatest producers in rap and hip-hop history. Most recently, he started a movie production company and released what he is calling his final studio album.

Eminem

Marshall Mathers, better known as Eminem, is an accomplished producer and one of the best selling rap artists of all time. He has won several Grammy Awards, as well as an Academy Award for his music.

Fergie

Born Stacy Ann Ferguson, Fergie is a solo artist and a vocalist for the hip-hop group Black Eyed Peas. She is one of the most accomplished female artists in music. Her first solo album produced six hit singles and sold more than six million

After spending years in the underground rap scene, Detroit native Eminem rose to fame with the release of his first Interscope-affiliated album, The Slim Shady LP, in 1999. Dr. Dre, his mentor, produced and appeared in some of Eminem's biggest hits. They collaborated on at least two notable singles, Eminem's "Guilty Conscience" and Dr. Dre's "Forgot About Dre."

50 Cent

Curtis Jackson raps under the stage name 50 Cent. Like Eminem, he is one of the best selling rap artists of all time. 50 Cent has also enjoyed success as an actor, writer, and entrepreneur.

The Ying Yang Twins

Mr. Collipark, the man who introduced Soulja Boy to Interscope Records, is also a multi-platinum producer for the Ying Yang Twins. The Ying Yang Twins are Kaine and D-Roc, an Atlanta-based rap duo best known for their feel-good party songs. Kaine and D-Roc started out as solo artists but decided to band together after being introduced by a mutual friend in 1996.

The Ying Yang Twins are sometimes credited with helping introduce the crunk **genre** of rap to the mainstream public. Although crunk is believed to have originated in the early 1990s, it did not become popular with a national audience until 2003.

The Ying Yang Twins started out on the club circuit and became local favorites. Their first single, "Whistle While You Twurk," received national airplay and brought attention to the group.

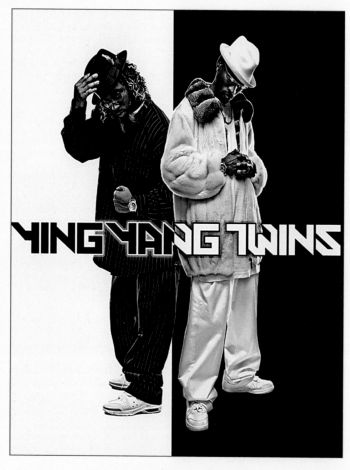

The Ying Yang Twins helped popularize crunk music in "Get Low," their 2003 collaboration with Lil Jon and the Eastside Boyz. They also worked with Britney Spears in 2003, introducing a still-wider audience to the repetitive, energetic style of crunk. Their other hits include "Wait (The Whisper Song)" and "Badd," both produced by Mr. Collipark.

Within three years, they had released two full-length albums and appeared on another album with Lil Jon. It was the guest appearance on Lil Jon's song "Get Low" that launched the Ying Yang Twins into superstardom.

Since then, the group has released six more successful albums and collaborated with a number of other famous artists.

(Go back to page 18.)

Female Hip-Hop Artists

Some of the most influential women in hip-hop include these artists:

Salt-n-Pepa

Salt-n-Pepa is the highest selling female rap group of all time. Members include Cheryl James (Salt), Sandra Denton (Pepa), and DJ Deidra Roper (Spinderella). Together, these three women are considered hip-hop pioneers.

MC Lyte

MC Lyte, born Lana Michele Moorer, is one of the first solo female rap artists to achieve real fame. She has sold millions of records worldwide and is frequently credited with paving the way for other female rappers.

Queen Latifah

Dana Elaine Owens, better known as Queen Latifah, is a Grammy Award-winning rap artist. She definitely helped blaze a trail for other women in hip-hop during the 1980s. Queen Latifah still enjoys success today in the music industry and as an actress and model.

Missy Elliot

Missy Elliot is an award-winning rapper and record producer. She is the only female rapper so far to have six certified platinum albums. Missy is also well known for the work she does with various charities.

Ciara

Ciara Princess Harris, who goes by her first name only, is part of the new generation of hip-hop. She has earned quite a few awards and nominations already, including a Grammy Award and an American Music Award. Ciara is also an accomplished actress and record producer.

Rapper Missy "Misdemeanor" Elliott has won five Grammy Awards and sold more than 7 million albums. Since 1997, she has released catchy, creative songs accompanied by technologically impressive videos. She has also written and produced hits for a number of other artists in a variety of genres, from soul to pop to hip-hop.

(Go back to page 31.)

Southern Hip-Hop

Southern hip-hop is one of the many different genres of American hip-hop music. Some people say that Southern hip-hop is responsible for the new hip-hop trends we see today.

What Makes It Different?

There are lots of things that make Southern hip-hop stand out from genres like East Coast and West Coast hip-hop. One of the most noticeable differences is the **tempo** of the music. Southern hip-hop usually has between 140 and 180 beats per minute. East Coast and West Coast hip-hop typically feature 90 to 120 beats per minute—a much slower tempo.

The Rise of Southern Hip-Hop

Some sub-genres of southern hip-hop, such as Dirty South rap and Miami Bass, have been popular since the early 1980s. But mainstream acceptance didn't come easy for other sub-genres, like Crunk and Southern Hardcore rap. It was in the late 1990s when the South became known for producing chart-topping hip-hop artists.

Notable Southern Hip-Hop Artists

2 Live Crew
Arrested Development
DJ Screw
Geto Boys
Goodie Mob
Khia
Lil Jon
Lil Scrappy
Lil Wayne
Ludacris
Master P
OutKast
Scarface
Soulja Boy Tell 'Em
Three 6 Mafia
Trick Daddy
Trina
UGK
Ying Yang Twins
Young Buck

Atlanta-based hip-hop artist Chris "Ludacris" Bridges performs exuberant, explicit music with strong Southern roots. In the late 1990s, Ludacris gained a local reputation as a radio DJ and an independent rapper. But he achieved worldwide fame in the early 2000s as one of the first Dirty South–style rappers to find mainstream success.

(Go back to page 34.)

Hip-Hop Fashion

Rapper Jay-Z's fashion sense evolves with the times. Here, he wears the sports gear popular among hip-hop artists in the 1990s. In recent years, his style has changed. As a co-founder of the popular clothing and accessory label Rocawear, Jay-Z exerts a strong influence over the hip-hop world's fashion as well as its music.

Fashion is a big part of hip-hop culture. Clothes, shoes, and jewelry are all used by artists and fans alike to convey style and expression. Although hip-hop fashion has changed over the years, it continues to influence popular fashion around the world.

1980s Hip-Hop Fashion

Back in the day, hip-hop artists wore a lot of tracksuits and heavy gold jewelry. Bright colors, oversized glasses, and belts with enormous name plates were also common in the 1980s.

1990s Hip-Hop Fashion

Sportswear was huge in the 1990s. Jackets, tennis shoes, and baseball caps were considered the height of hip-hop fashion. Rappers also began to wear baggy pants without belts. Letting their pants sag was a style in itself.

Modern Hip-Hop Fashion

Some hip-hop artists still embrace baggy clothes and sportswear. Others opt for form-fitting clothing or a more preppy style of dress. A "bling culture" is also present, meaning that a significant number of hip-hop artists wear platinum and silver jewelry or accessories imbedded with diamonds and other precious gems.

Fashion Labels and Clothing Lines

There are quite a few hip-hop artists and executives who create and wear their own fashion labels and clothing lines. A few notable examples include the following:

50 Cent	Ludacris
Biggy Smalls	Nelly
Busta Rhyme	OutKast
Diddy	Russell Simmons
DMX	Snoop Dogg
Eminem	Tupac Shakur
Jay-Z	Young Jeezy
Kimora Lee Simmons	

(Go back to page 40.)

Hip-Hop Artists in Films

Soulja Boy Tell 'Em has expressed an interest in acting. If he decides to pursue this passion, he won't be the only hip-hop-artist-turned-movie-star. Some of the most popular names in hip-hop have made it to the screen:

Will Smith

After rising to fame as The Fresh Prince, Will Smith became one of the biggest TV and movie stars in the world. He is one of only three actors to have seven consecutive movies make more than $100 million at the box office.

Ice Cube

Ice Cube is regarded as one of the greatest rappers ever, but making music isn't his only talent. He is also a writer, director, producer, and movie star. To date, he has appeared in nearly 30 movies.

Snoop Dogg

Best known as a rapper on the West Coast hip-hop scene, Snoop Dogg has also appeared in his fair share of movies. Most recently, he had his own reality TV show and a recurring cameo role on the soap opera *One Life to Live*.

Ice-T

After helping pioneer gangsta rap, Ice-T embarked on a serious acting career. He has

Will Smith (right) in the 1996 movie Bad Boys, with co-star Martin Lawrence. Will Smith originally played humorous roles, which matched the family-friendly rap he recorded as the Fresh Prince, but his dramatic performances have won critical praise as well. He has earned two Academy Award nominations for Best Actor: for 2001's Ali and for 2006's The Pursuit of Happyness.

had notable lead performances in everything from comedies and dramas to horror movies. Probably best known for his role in *Law and Order: Special Victims Unit*, Ice-T has also done lots of voice-over work for popular video games. (Go back to page 47.) ◀◀

Selected Highlights

1973   Kool Herc deejays his first party at 1520 Sedgwick Avenue, Bronx, New York.

1974   Grandmaster Caz and Grandmaster Flash begin to DJ their own parties.

1975   DJ GrandWizzard Theodore accidentally invents the scratch technique on his turntable.

1979   "Rapper's Delight," a single from the Sugar Hill Gang, reaches number 36 on the Billboard Hot 100.

1982   Afrika Bambaataa and the Soul Sonic Force use new synthesizer technology to create "Planet Rock," one of the first hip-hop songs to incorporate an electronic sound.

1984   Russell Simmons and Rick Rubin launch the pioneer hip-hop label Def Jam Records.

1988   N.W.A. releases *Straight Outta Compton*, one of the earliest and most influential West Coast hip-hop albums.

1990   DeAndre Cortez Way (Soulja Boy Tell 'Em) is born on July 28 in Chicago, Illinois.

2003   After moving to Atlanta at the age of six and then to Mississippi to live with his father, Soulja Boy Tell 'Em discovers the Internet.

2004   Soulja Boy Tell 'Em launches his own record label, Stacks on Deck Entertainment.

2005   Soulja Boy Tell 'Em begins rapping and posting songs on YouTube and other Web sites.

2006   Soulja Boy Tell 'Em records the independently produced album, *Unsigned and Still Major*.

2007   "Crank That" reaches number one on the Billboard Hot 100. *Souljaboytellem.com* is released.

2008   *Forbes* names Soulja Boy Tell 'Em the "Hottest New Music Star."

Singles

2006   "Bapes"

2007   "Crank That (Soulja Boy)"
"Soulja Girl"

2008   "Yahhh!"
"Let Me Get 'Em"
"Donk"
"iDance"

Guest Appearances

2007   "Clumsy (Collipark Remix)"
"Girlfriend"

2008   "Get It Poppin"
"They Lookin' At My Neck"
"Get Silly"
"My Dougie (Remix)"
"Kaveman"

Albums

2007   *Unsigned and Still Major*
Souljaboytellem.com

Select Awards

2007   Ozone's Patiently Waiting Award
Dirty Award for Best Dance Song
BET Award for Best Hip-Hop Dance
Grammy Nomination for Best Rap Song
BET's Top Music Video

2008   *Forbes* Hottest New Music Star

Books

Chang, Jeff, and D.J. Kool Herc. *Can't Stop Won't Stop: A History of the Hip-hop Generation*. New York: Picador, 2005.

Kearse, Randy. *Street Talk: Da Official Guide to Hip-Hop & Urban Slanguage*. Fort Lee, N.J.: Barricade Books, 2007.

Neal, Mark Anth. *That's the Joint!: Hip-Hop Studies Reader*. New York: Routledge, 2004.

Ogbar, Jeffrey O.G. *Hip-Hop Revolution: The Culture and Politics of Rap*. Lawrence: University Press of Kansas, 2007.

Wells, Peggy Sue. *Soulja Boy*. Hockessin, Del.: Mitchell Lane Publishers, 2008.

Web Sites

http://souljaboytellem.com
The official Web site of Soulja Boy Tell 'Em features a blog, photos, and videos, as well as information about tour dates and appearances.

http://www.myspace.com/souljaboytellem
Soulja Boy Tell 'Em's official MySpace page features general information about Soulja Boy Tell 'Em, as well as photos, tour dates, and videos.

http://www.youtube.com
The official YouTube Web site offers access to hundreds of Soulja Boy Tell 'Em music videos and interviews.

http://music.aol.com
The official AOL Web site has an entire section devoted to Soulja Boy Tell 'Em that includes a bio, songs, videos, photos, and much more.

http://www.souljaboystore.com
Interscope Records provides a Soulja Boy Tell 'Em store on this Web site. Fans can buy and make their own t-shirts, sunglasses, posters, and CDs.

Publisher's note:
The Web sites mentioned in this book were active at the time of publication. The publisher is not responsible for Web sites that have changed their addresses or discontinued operation since the date of publication. The publisher will review and update the Web site addresses each time the book is reprinted.

beats—in hip-hop music, sounds that recur at regular intervals.

controversy—something that inspires differing opinions, debate, or disputes.

culture—the beliefs, practices, and forms of expression, such as art, language, literature, music, and fashion, that characterize or represent a group of people.

cut—in scratching, to create a special musical effect by capturing the sound of the forward scratch of a record on the turntable and using a fader, or switch, to shut out the sound of the backward scratch.

denigration—the act of belittling or saying something bad about someone.

domestically—within the country of origin.

entrepreneur—an individual who starts a business or enterprise.

genre—a category or kind of music.

groove—a quality that is associated with rhythm-and-blues and soul music that gives a satisfying rhythm to the music, such as a beat that makes it easy to dance to.

impromptu—unplanned; spur of the moment.

label—a company that issues musical recordings under a trademarked name.

one-hit wonder—an artist who only has one hit song.

parody—an imitation of something that mocks or pokes fun at the thing it imitates.

ringbacks—the noises heard by calling parties after dialing a mobile number.

ringtones—sounds made by mobile phones to indicate incoming calls.

tag—a signature; in graffiti, the symbols or characters used to identify a particular artist and his or her work.

tempo—a measure used to describe the rate of speed in music.

tracks—songs on an album.

unprecedented—having never happened before.

viral marketing—a form of marketing that encourages other people to promote something via word of mouth.

page 9   "'Crank That' was just . . . " *Soulja Boy Tell 'Em Interview* (Alloy.com: http://www.alloy.com/5/86/7012/1/ref/5/86/7012/7/more_module_spot_6_link, 2007).

page 11   "When I started rapping . . . " *Soulja Boy Tell 'Em Interview* (Alloy.com: http://www.alloy.com/5/86/7012/1/ref/5/86/7012/7/more_module_spot_6_link, 2007).

page 12   "He was the one . . . " *Soulja Boy Tell 'Em Official Bio* (Souljaboytellem.com: http://www.souljaboytellem.com/-/Main.aspx?pbt_name=Bio, 2008).

page 13   "When I went to . . . " *Soulja Boy Tell 'Em Official Bio*, http://www.souljaboytellem.com/-/Main.aspx?pbt_name=Bio.

page 14   "Really I was just . . . " Hillary Crosley, *Ready for Duty: Online Fame Leads Soulja Boy to Radio* (New York: Billboard, 2007), 70.

page 18   "The most exciting moment . . . " *Soulja Boy Tell 'Em Interview*, http://www.alloy.com/5/86/7012/1/ref/5/86/7012/7/more_module_spot_6_link.

page 18   "The more I'm around . . . " *Soulja Boy Tell 'Em Official Bio*, http://www.souljaboytellem.com/-/Main.aspx?pbt_name=Bio.

page 23   "They've got it all . . . " Daniel Kilkelly, *Soulja Boy Insists Songs Aren't Sexual* (Digital Spy: http://www.digitalspy.co.uk/music/a92106/soulja-boy-insists-songs-arent-sexual.html, 2008).

page 25   "That's how I was . . . " Kilkelly, *Soulja Boy Insists Songs Aren't Sexual*, http://www.digitalspy.co.uk/music/a92106/soulja-boy-insists-songs-arent-sexual.html.

page 28   "They'll say I opened . . . " Jayson Rodriguez, with reporting by Tim Kash, Soulja Boy Claims He's The Hottest MC In the Game—Better Than Jay-Z, Kanye . . . (MTV.com: http://www.mtv.com/news/articles/1579947/20080118/soulja_boy_tellem.jhtml#, 2008).

page 34   "Hip-hop is not . . . " Shake, Don Imus: The Hip-hop Community Responds (Hiphopdx.com: http://www.hiphopdx.com/index/news/id.5132/p.all/print.true, 2007).

page 37   "They're not making substance . . . " Associated Press, *Huge Hits Don't Spell Success for New Rap Stars* (MSNBC: http://www.msnbc.msn.com/id/21365044/, 2007).

page 37   "He has a better . . . " *Soulja Boy Tell 'Em Official Bio*, http://www.souljaboytellem.com/-/Main.aspx?pbt_name=Bio.

page 40   "In this business, you . . . " John Benson, *Soulja Boy Rides Wave of Fame and Doesn't Take It for Granted*, (Vindy.com: http://www.vindy.com/news/2008/jan/24/soulja-boy-rides-wave-of-fame-and-doesn8217t/, 2008).

page 42   "It's been an incredible . . . " Hillary Crosley, *Soulja Boy Hitting The Road With Lil' Mama* (Billboard.com: http://www.billboard.com/bbcom/news/article_display.jsp?vnu_content_id=1003726677, 2008).

page 43   "I'd say coming into . . . " *John Soeder, Riding Dance Craze, Soulja Boy Cranks into 2008 with Tour* (Cleveland.com: http://www.cleveland.com/entertainment/index.ssf/2008/01/riding_dance_craze_soulja_boy.html, 2008).

page 45   "My new album is . . . " Shaheem Reid, *Soulja Boy Tell'em Goes Back To School, Hopes To Collaborate With Chris Brown* (MTV.com: http://www.mtv.com/news/articles/1586436/20080428/soulja_boy_tellem.jhtml#, 2008).

Numbers in **bold italics** refer to captions.

Karen Schweitzer has written numerous articles for magazines, newspapers, and Web sites like About.com. She has also authored several books for young adults, including biographies of Shaun White, Sheryl Swoopes, and Tyra Banks. Karen lives in Michigan with her husband. You can learn more about her at www.karenschweitzer.com.

PICTURE CREDITS

page

1: Interscope Records/PRMS
4: Interscope Records/PRMS
7: Soulja Boy Tell 'Em/PRMS
8: Virgin Media/PRMS
10: Soulja Boy Tell 'Em/PRMS
12: RCA Music Group/NMI
15: Stacks On Deck Ent./NMI
16: Soulja Boy Tell 'Em/PRMS
19: Soulja Boy Tell 'Em/PRMS
20: R. Hagans/CIC Photos
23: Seth Browarnik/WireImage
24: The Source/NMI
26: Moses Robinson/WireImage
29: WireImage
30: Gary James/WENN Photos
32: Music Alive/NMI

33: London Records/NMI
35: AFP Photos
36: Interscope Records/PRMS
38: Interscope Records/PRMS
41: Soulja Boy Tell 'Em/PRMS
43: Jaston/IOA Photos
44: Ken Goff Photos
46: Mark Allan/WireImage
48: T&T/IOA Photos
49: Billboard/NMI
51: S. Lispi/BWPhoto
52: TVT Records/PRMS
53: VH1/AdMedia
54: AdMedia/Sipa Press
55: Def Jam Records/NMI
56: Columbia Pictures/NMI

Front cover: Interscope Records/PRMS